Wid
Starters
Blue Book 1

Phyllis Flowerdew

Tze Hong Yee (謝巨頤)

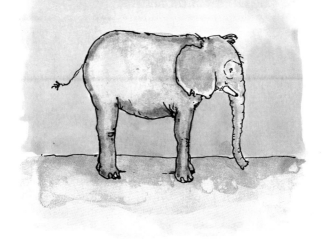

Oliver & Boyd

Acknowledgment

'The Number of Spots' was adapted, with permission, from a story of the same name in *The Long Grass Whispers* by Geraldine Elliot (© Geraldine Elliot 1949), published by Routledge & Kegan Paul Ltd.

Illustrated by Nancy Bryce, Kate Canning, Annabel Large, Maggie Ling, and Harry Horse

Oliver & Boyd
Robert Stevenson House
1-3 Baxter's Place
Leith Walk
Edinburgh EH1 3BB

A Division of Longman Group UK Ltd

First published 1985
Fourth impression 1989

ISBN 0 05 003686 6

Set in 16/24 point Monophoto Plantin
Produced by Longman Group (FE) Ltd
Printed in Hong Kong

Where to find the Stories

Page

4 Shaggy and the Fire

12 Why the Bear has a Short Tail

19 The Jumble Sale

28 The Jumping Bed

39 The Number of Spots

Shaggy and the Fire

"It's a cold day,"
said Shaggy's mother,
"and the fire has gone out.
Run, Shaggy,
to the Keeper of the Fire,
and ask him for a burning brand
to start our fire again."

"Yes Mother," said Shaggy.
"I will do that."

"Run as fast as you can,
and take great care,"
said Mother.

"Yes Mother," said Shaggy.
"I will do that."

So Shaggy ran very fast
until he came
to the Keeper of the Fire.

He saw the smoke
going up, up, up.
He saw the flames
leaping, leaping, leaping.
 "Our fire has gone out,"
he said to the Keeper of the Fire.
"Please may I have
a burning brand
to start it up again?"

"Here you are,"
said the Keeper of the Fire.
"Run as fast as you can,
and take great care."

"Thank you," said Shaggy.
He held the burning brand
and he ran very fast
and he took great care.

Then a little wind blew.

"I will blow out
your burning brand," it said,
and it blew and it blew.
But Shaggy hid quickly
in an open cave,
and kept the brand burning.
And when he came out
the wind had gone.

Then he ran on.
He ran very fast
and he took great care.

Soon the wind blew again.

"I will blow out
your burning brand," it said,
and it blew and it blew.
But Shaggy hid quickly
in a little wood,
and kept the brand burning.
And when he came out
the wind had gone.

Then he ran on.
He ran very fast
and he took great care.

Soon the wind blew again.

"I will blow out
your burning brand," it said,
and it blew and it blew.
But Shaggy hid quickly
behind a big rock,

and kept the brand burning.
And when he came out,
the wind had gone.

Then he ran on.
He ran very fast
and he took great care.

Soon the wind blew again.
"I will blow out
your burning brand," it said.
"NO YOU WILL NOT,"
said Shaggy,
"for here is my home
and here is our fire
waiting to be lit."

Quickly
he pushed the burning brand
into the dead fire,
and at once

a little smoke began
to go up and up,
and flames went
leaping, leaping into the sky.

"Good boy, Shaggy,"
said Mother.
"Now we shall soon
be warm again."

The smoke went up and up.
The sticks went crackle,
crackle, crackle.
The flames went
leaping, leaping into the sky.
And the wind blew away
the way he had come.

Why the Bear has a Short Tail

This is a very old story.

One day, in a cold, north land,
a pile of fish
fell off a sledge
and lay in the snow.
The man who was driving the sledge
didn't turn round,
so he didn't know
that he had lost the fish.
He just went on his way,
on and on, over the snow.

Soon a fox came along,
and saw the pile of fish
lying on the snow.

"Ah!" he said.   "Fish!
Just what I like!"
He started to eat the fish.
He ate one, two, three.
He ate four, five, six.
Now there were only a few left.

When he had eaten
nearly all of them,
a bear came along.
He had a long, fluffy tail,
as all bears had in those days.

"Ah!" he said.   "Fish!
Just what I like.
Where did you get them?"

"I caught them," said the fox.

"Where?" asked the bear.

"In the river," said the fox.

"But the river is thick with ice,"
said the bear.

"I will tell you what to do,"
said the fox.

"You must bang the ice
with a stone,
and make a hole in it.
Then you must sit
with your back to the river
and your tail in the hole.
You must wait a little while,
and soon you will feel the fish
bite your tail.
Then you can pull them up,
one by one."

"Thank you," said the bear.
"I will do that."

So the bear went to the river.
He banged the ice
with a stone,
and made a hole in it.
Then he sat
with his back to the river,
and his tail in the hole,
as the fox had told him to do.

He waited,
and he waited,
and he waited,
but no fish came.
He waited,
and he waited,
and he waited,
but still no fish came.
He grew colder
and colder,
and colder,
and even then,
no fish came.

He grew so cold
that he could not sit there
any longer.
"That bad fox has tricked me,"
he said.
"There are no fish here."

He tried to jump up,
but his tail was frozen into the ice.
He pulled and pulled,
but he could not get free.
He pulled and pulled again,
but still he could not get free.
Then he gave a great tug,
a great BIG tug,
and he was free at last.
But most of his tail
was left behind in the ice.

And that, so people say,
is why the bear
has such a short tail today. *Adapted*

The Jumble Sale

It was Saturday.
There was a jumble sale
in the Church hall.
Sally and her mother
were helping.
They had a lot of things to sell.
There were jerseys
and jeans
and shirts.

There were dresses
and blouses
and skirts.
There were shoes
and boots
and wellingtons,
and there was an old jacket
of Dad's.

"I'm sure that will soon sell,"
said Sally.

At two o'clock
Sally opened the doors,
and people rushed
into the hall.

They picked up jerseys
    and jeans
    and shirts.
They looked at dresses
    and blouses
    and skirts.
They tried on shoes
    and boots
    and wellingtons.
    "How much is this?" asked a lady,
holding up Dad's jacket.
Sally told her the price.

"I'll have it, please,"
said the lady.
She gave Sally the money,
and went out of the hall
with the jacket over her arm.
  "That was soon sold,"
said Mum.

The jumble sale went on.
Sally and her mother
sold more and more things,
and put more and more money
into the box.

"Soon there won't be anything left,"
said Sally.

Just then Dad came in.
He looked very upset.

"Didn't you go
to watch the football?"
asked Mum.

"Where's my jacket?" said Dad.

"You gave it to us to bring," said Mum. "It's sold now."

"It's gone," said Sally.

"Oh dear, oh dear," said Dad. "Who did you sell it to?"

"A lady," said Sally.

"Who was it?" asked Dad.

"I don't know," said Sally. "I've never seen her before."

"Oh dear, oh dear," said Dad again. "I left some money in the pocket.

It was thirty pounds
for the rent.
We must get the jacket back."
But how could they get it back?
How? How? How?
Lots of people had left the hall.
Many had gone home
in a bus or a car.
How could Dad get his jacket back?

At three o'clock
most things had been sold.
At four o'clock
everything had been sold.
"We must clear up now,"
said Mum,
"and lock the doors again."

Just then a lady came
into the hall.
She was holding Dad's jacket.
"I went all the way home,"
she said,
"and then I found this
in the pocket."
She held up some money.
It was thirty pounds,
thirty pounds for the rent!
So everything ended happily
just in time.

The Jumping Bed

Candy had a new bed.
Her mother tucked her up in it,
and said goodnight.

Candy closed her eyes
and fell asleep
almost at once.

Soon her mother and father
and her brother Tom
went to bed too.

The house was quiet
and dark and still.
   Then suddenly
Candy awoke with a start.
The bed had jumped!
She was sure the bed had jumped!

"It must have been a dream,"
she thought.

But no!
The bed jumped again.
It jumped again
and again and again.
It jumped and it shook
all the night long,
and poor Candy
had hardly any sleep at all.

At breakfast time
Mother said,
   "Did you have a good night
in your new bed, Candy?"
   "No," said Candy.
"It jumped all night,
and I had hardly any sleep at all."
   "How can a bed jump?"
said her father,
but Candy began to cry.
   "I'll try it tonight,"
said Tom.
"Perhaps it won't jump with me."
   So that night
Candy slept in Tom's bed,
and Tom slept in the new one.
He closed his eyes,
and fell asleep
almost at once.

Soon Mother and Father and Candy
went to bed too.

The house was quiet
and dark and still.

Then suddenly
Tom awoke with a start.
The bed had jumped!
He was sure the bed had jumped!
"It must have been a dream,"
he thought.
But no!
The bed jumped again.
It jumped again
and again and again.
It jumped and it shook
all the night long,
and poor Tom
had hardly any sleep at all.

At breakfast time
Mother said,
    "Well Tom,
did you have a good night
in Candy's new bed?"
    "No," said Tom.
"It jumped all night,
and I had hardly any sleep at all."
    "How can a bed jump?"
said Father.
"I'll try it tonight.
I'm sure it won't jump
with me."

So that night
Father slept in the new bed.
He closed his eyes
and fell asleep
almost at once.

Mother and Candy and Tom
went to bed too.
The house was quiet
and dark and still.

Then suddenly
Father awoke with a start.
The bed had jumped!

He was sure the bed had jumped!

"It must have been a dream,"
he thought.

But no!
The bed jumped again.
It jumped again
and again and again.
It jumped and it shook
all the night long,
and poor Father
had hardly any sleep at all.

At breakfast time
Mother said,
    "Well, did the bed jump
last night?"
    "Yes," said Father crossly.
"It jumped all night,
and I had hardly any sleep at all.
The children are quite right.
It IS a jumping bed,
and I am going to the shop today
to ask the man to change it."

So the jumping bed
went back to the shop,
and the shop man sent it back
to the factory.

But no one ever found out
why it jumped
or what the factory did with it
in the end.

R.E. MOVE
Strange bed removers
10 Uphill road,
Downhill,
Roundabout

As for Candy,
the shop sent a new bed for her.
It was not too hard
and not too soft,
and it never, never jumped
or shook at all.
So Candy slept happily in it
every night, all night long.

THINGS
GO BUMP IN
THE NIGHT
&
OTHER JUMPY
STORIES
BY MAGGIE LING

The Number of Spots

Leopard was very proud of his spots.
  "I wonder how many there are,"
he said.
He didn't know how to count them,
so he asked Crocodile.
  "Crocodile," he said,
"will you please
count my spots for me?"
  "Oh no," said Crocodile.
"I don't want to waste my time,"
but really he didn't know
how to count.

So Leopard asked Wart-hog.

"Wart-hog," he said,
"will you please count my spots
for me?"

"Count them?" said Wart-hog.
"Do you mean one, two, three, four?"

"Yes, that's right,"
said Leopard.
"I'm so glad you know how to count."

"I don't know how to count,"
said Wart-hog.
"I only know that I've got four legs.
I don't know what comes after four."

So Leopard asked Elephant.

"Elephant," he said,

"will you count my spots for me?"

"Yes," said Elephant kindly,

and he began,

"One, two, three, four, five,

six, seven, eight, nine, ten."

"Isn't he clever?"

said the other animals,

but Elephant was going on,

"One, two, three, four, five,

six, seven, eight, nine, ten,"
all over again.

"You did up to ten,"
said the other animals.
"There are lots more numbers after ten."

"Oh I don't bother with those,"
said Elephant.
"I've counted two tens.
That makes twenty.
Leopard has more than twenty spots."
And Elephant walked away
because he couldn't really
count more than ten.

So Leopard asked Ant-bear.

"Ant-bear," he said,
"will you please count my spots
for me?"

"Yes," said Ant-bear kindly,
"but I can't count more than fifty,"
and she began,

"One, two, three, four, five,
six, seven, eight, nine, ten."
She went on and on
until she came to twenty-nine.

"I can't remember
what comes after twenty-nine,"
she said.

"Is it thirty or forty?"
asked Tortoise.

"Oh yes, thirty,"
said Ant-bear.
"Thank you, Tortoise."

But now she had lost her place.

"I don't know which spot
I'm up to," she said.

"This one," said Elephant,
who had come back again.

"No, this one," said Wart-hog.

"Oh dear," said Ant-bear.
"I shall have to start
all over again."

Just then up came Rabbit.

"What are you doing?" he asked.

"Leopard wants someone
to count his spots,"
said Ant-bear.

"I'll count them," said Rabbit kindly.
He started counting the spots
one by one,
and saying something in a whisper.
The animals thought
he was saying the numbers,
but really he was saying,
"dark, light, dark, light."
He touched every single spot.
It took a long, long time.

Then he said,

"Leopard has two spots."

"Two spots!" said everyone.

"He must have more than two!"

"No," said Rabbit, "just two.

He has dark ones and light ones."

"But how MANY?" asked the animals.

"How many spots?"

"Oh," said Rabbit.
"I thought you wanted to know
how many SORTS of spots.
There are two sorts,
dark and light."
Then he hopped away.

"Oh dear," said Leopard sadly,
and he never did know
how many spots he had after all.

Adapted

48